SOLDIER BOY
(IN PEACE TIME?)

AN ARMY VETERAN'S MEMORIES

FRANK DI GIACOMO

Copyright ©2025, Frank Di Giacomo

ALL RIGHTS RESERVED.

No part of this publication may be reproduced, stored in a retrieval system, or transmitted in any form or by any means—electronic, mechanical, photo-copy, recording, or any other—except for brief quotation in reviews, without the prior permission of the author or publisher.

ISBN: 978-1-962402-25-5

Published by

Fideli Publishing, Inc.
119 W. Morgan St.
Martinsville, IN 46151
www.FideliPublishing.com

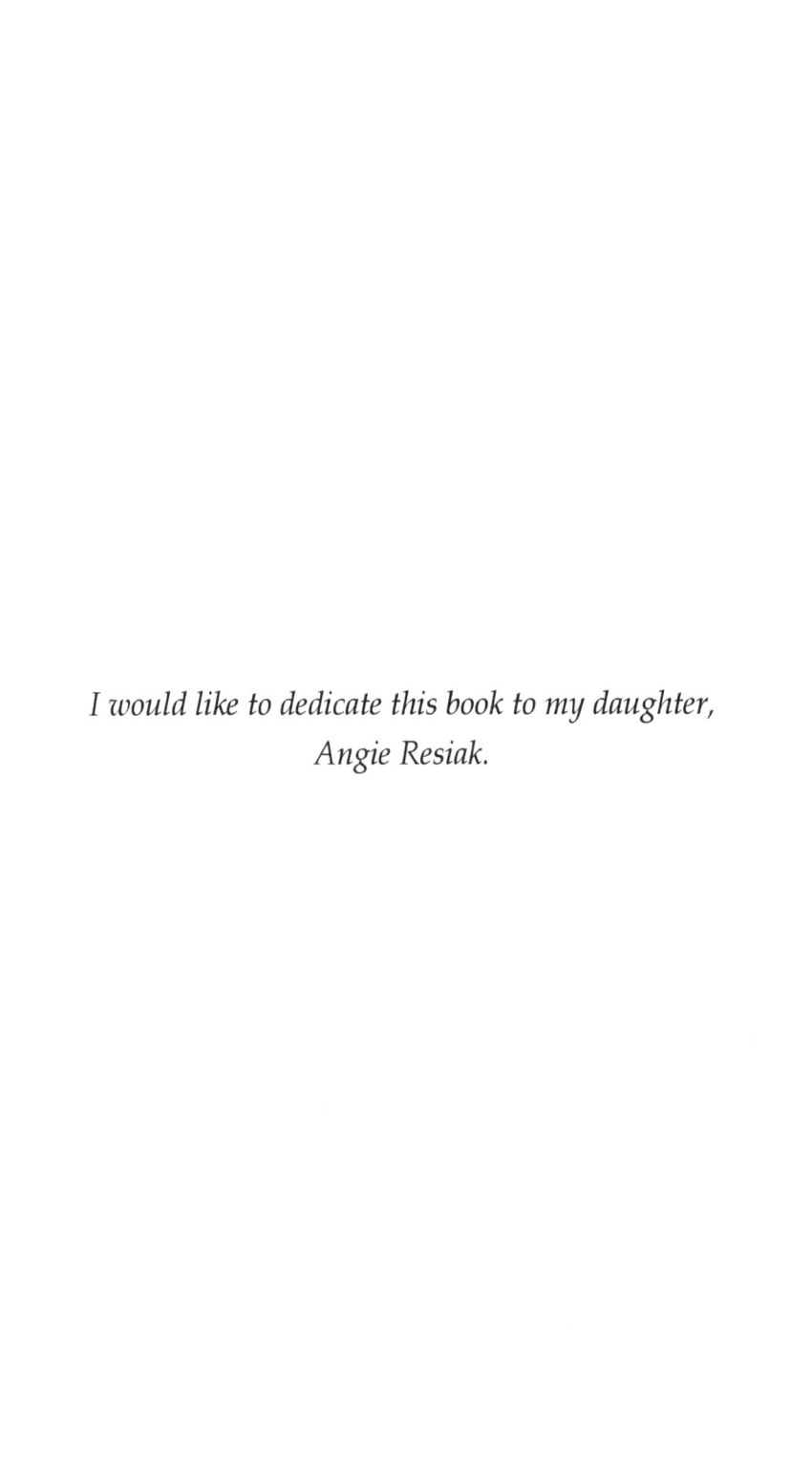

*I would like to dedicate this book to my daughter,
Angie Resiak.*

About the Author

I was born in Ozone Park, New York, and lived there for six years, then moved with my parents to Fall River Massachusetts. Eventually, I moved to Michigan City, Indiana, and I'm still here. My achievements were in engineering and the arts.

You're in the Army Now

After my pre-induction in to the U.S. Army, I thought I had better choose a service before the choice was made for me, so I picked the Navy Air. A month later, I drove to Notre Dame for my test. I got there early, and boy I was nervous. I asked myself, *Do I belong here?*

Suddenly the door opened and in came a group of well-dressed cadets. *Oh shit!* My heart just about stopped. *Oh well,* I thought, *all I can do now is my best!*

The test took about an hour. I finished early so I revied my work. When everyone was done, our tests were scored. Guess what? I flunked!

I was ready to get the hell out of there but I was also curious. So, I asked the instructor, "How bad did I do?" To my surprise, he said I missed it by 10 points, and had the class been made up of men off the street instead of the cadets I would have passed! I didn't think that was too bad, since I hadn't taken an academic route in high school, preferring vocational training instead.

Prior to this test, a neighbor of mine, a Navy Lieutenant Commander during WWII, and I were invited to the Great Lakes Naval base. We had dinner and then I met all the officers. It felt great being part of this gathering.

OK, I thought, it's too late to choose a service, *I'm screwed!* I soon got my draft notice that said to direct my body to where I could catch the military bus. It was June 3, 1959, and my destination was the 5th Army Induction Center in Chicago, Illinois.

If you're a modest soul, you'd find the induction process difficult. There we all were, standing in line, naked with our legs spread

Soldier Boy in Peace Time

apart, ready for short-arm inspection[1] and all. I made the mistake of turning around and saw a guy who was dripping puss from a wound. That made my stomach flip! Anyway, long story short, I passed my physical.

After this, those of us who passed were headed for basic training at Ft. Lenardwood, Missouri. Lucky me, I ended up on a train with a Pullman sleeper. How about that!

When we arrived, to my surprise it looked just like a 1942 camp with a wood burning stove! I'd heard it was hot and humid here in the summer, which I would find out later was true.

Life here was certainly different. Every day we were picking up cigarette butts and I had KP duty for two weeks, but no basic training. I couldn't help but wonder, what was going on. Finaly, after two weeks, we were told that they

---

1 A "short-arm inspection" is a military euphemism referring to the routine medical inspection of male soldiers' penises (short arms).

were full here and we would have to move to Ft. Hood in Texas!

We made it to camp in Texas in late June and boy was it hot —*110 degrees!* After three days, we were again told the facility was full. *What now?* I wondered. Oh no, just my luck, the Rangers mustered out, so guess who was next. Yes, that would be my group.

The first thing we did was practice crawling under a 50-caliber machinegun as it fired. That was nerve racking, and it certainly wasn't anything like they show in the movies. It was loud and scary, but then when we practiced at night, the tracers looked like they were coming right at you. (*Hell, that was twice as scary!*)

The highlight of my time here was when I had grenade training. We had to go and handle one dummy and three live grenades. The A grenade has a pin and a lever. The pin releases a chemical and the lever releases the 4-second timer. Now here's where I acted up. I went to throw the live grenade and my Seargent's eyes popped because I waited two seconds before I let it go! I wanted to throw more, but he told me to get the hell out of there, I was disappointed because I really enjoyed it!

The thing I hated the most was bayonet practice. When a knife with the sheave off comes at you, it's nerve-racking. I also knew there'd been accidents.

For example, in the confidence course we had targets standing and we had loaded M1 rifles. There was a guy behind me who wasn't paying attention. He had his rifle pointed at my back with his finger on the trigger and the safety off! Good thing the Sergeant caught that! Boy did he give that guy hell!

Bivouac is where a solider goes camping, sort of. Each soldier carries half of a shelter on their back, and when they get to where they're going they put two halves together to make one tent. My friend from Missouri said, "Jock, you find a spot." So, I did. Suddenly, he yelled, "Jock, freeze!" I stopped, looked down and realized I was standing in the middle of a snake pit! All around me were venomous snakes, and one was frighteningly close to my leg! I slowly moved back with my heart trying to exit my body through my mouth!

After running back to report the incident to the snake killers, one of them mentioned that a snake was resting on my duffle bag! *They must love me*, I thought. *Is this a bad omen?* Ha ha!

The thing is, they never hissed or rattled. It was like they didn't care that I was there.

After this excitement, we went to an outside bar where the biggest locust I'd ever seen were flying around us! You could actually feel them kick when they left your shoulder! It's true, everything really is BIG in Texas!

Oh, I forgot to mention that Elvis Presley visited this place. His name was carved on the wall in the field outhouse. Yes, he was here a year before me. And it's true he didn't want any special treatment.

The next thing I faced was a large tower with a rope going down to six feet off the ground. I rushed to the tower and shimmied down. Or at least I tried to, but was blocked by a soldier

Soldier Boy in Peace Time

who froze halfway down the rope! I tried to talk him into moving, because my arms were getting tired.

So, me being strong and macho guy I am (ha-ha) I swung around him with one arm and then the other. I finally made it and jumped the final six feet down. The Ranger instructor just shook his head in disappointed at my less than stellar performance.

Next up was a 14-mile hike wearing a full field pack. Did I mention it was hot? On the way back, I was up front and everyone was tired and angry. So, when we stopped for a rest, we just flopped down anywhere — puddles, mud, it didn't matter.

On the way back to the barracks, a guy in the back of the line started complaining about me. I stopped the line and I lost it. I said, "Come up here and I'll knock the crap out of you!" My Missouri buddy tried to get me to cool down. I guess it was a good thing the guy shut up and didn't react to my threat. I'm not proud of that exchange.

On our last day, we did a few field maneuvers. The result for me was a scorpion who was not a friend — he nailed me good! It made me sick but I didn't want to go to sick bay on my last day, so my buddies took care of me.

The real down side to this was that five hours from being stung, I was supposed to be home getting married. You can see the big bandage on my finger in my wedding pictures.

After the wedding, I got orders to go to Ft. Bliss in Texas. I was excited to have my bride going with me. On the bus on the way there, there was a conflict and a sergeant was ordered to move to the back of the bus. Well, that didn't sit well with me. I exploded and said, "He's sitting with us!"

The sergeant said, "I'll move to the back. Please don't make any problems."

The landscape on the way to Ft. Bliss, which is in El Paso, was flat and dry but beautiful. The sunset lighting up that red clay plateau in the distance was amazing. Upon arriving, I checked in and then my wife and I went apartment hunting.

The song "El Paso" debuted on the radio at the same time we found our basement apartment. The owner and landlord was retired Air Force and his wife was from Germany. They were nice people and ended up being like family. My landlady, Ursula, got along great with my wife; both having German backgrounds. On Halloween, we would take her little daughter, Claudia, around the neighborhood to trick or treat. We just loved her.

My first day of work came and I was given the title Construction Draftsman MOS 811.10. I worked nights and drew up plans for the Nike Ajax Missile firing mechanism.

The area was interesting. There was a military school and grocery stores that had a nursery to keep the kids while you shopped. One time, on the radio, they said to come on down and paint the station building. That was fun! It was a progressive and interesting city.

On guard duty at night it's quiet and cold, but by noon it's hot! When you look up on the base of the mountain, you see the name Juarez. Also, when I had guard duty on the corner of the base, I had to salute the red plate (officer). Blue was for EM or enlisted men.

There was a time when I wanted to change my MOS to 814 ILLUSTRATOR. I tried, and took a little time doing the art. The civilian instructor let me go but then said he was sorry because the artwork turned out just great!

Korea Bound

It was required that all soldiers would have to serve overseas or in Germany or Korea! Well, with my luck, I got Korea! Oh, did I feel bad! Pryor to this I had put in for Germany. Ordinarily, you could appeal the decision, but my orders came down from higher ups, so I had no choice!

I'd miss Ft. Bliss. It was great — it had two pools, a theater, PX groceries and lots of activities.

Soldier Boy in Peace Time

I was worried about breaking the news to my wife, but she took it well. I think she wanted me out of her hair. He-he!

It seemed like I waited months to get my embarkation notice. It took so long that for a minute I felt like I was a civilian. Eventually it did come, and I got my bags packed (isn't there a song like dat?). Then, l said my goodbyes. Funny, no one cried, except me!

I boarded the flight ast Midway Airport in Chicago. From there, it was on to San Francisco — eight hours by prop plane.

What a hollow feeling I experienced, like I just went to a funeral for a loved one. I could feel the vibrations of the plane's props turning, and boy could you hear them. (Later, when I flew again, I still recalled that hollow feeling.)

The plane landed and I checked out, ready for embarkation. Then it was all-aboard time as I boarded the USS *Sultan*. The ship was full but everybody was pretty quiet. I ran and, eureka, I got to claim a bottom bunk!

I decided to put my civilian life out of my mind. My moto became, "You do what you have to do." Even so, I've got to say I got emotional when we passed under the Golden Gate Bridge.

Whoever said the Pacific was calm got it wrong. I love the ocean and was brought up near the Atlantic. I never get sea sick, but I came close to losing it when another soldier up-chucked in his plate at chow and the plate slid down in front of me as the ship was tossed around!

That was the end of my hunger, so I went out on deck and watched the waves coming over the bow. I turned and looked up at the bridge and waved to the skipper. He waved back, but I bet he was thinking I was some crazy solider.

I didn't like the practice where they shut the water-tight doors on the ship. One soldier kept saying we were on a submarine because the portholes were under the waterline.

Soldier Boy in Peace Time

Being close to Tokyo at 4 a.m., I saw the sun coming up. It looked just like the Japanese flag! That was awesome.

When it was sunny, everybody was on deck clowning around. We had butt cans for cigarettes. One day an AGI sat his big butt on a red can marked "butts." He got a million laughs from that stunt.

When we were on the Yellow Sea, to my surprise, the water realy was an olive drab yellowish color due the silt.

Finally, we reached Incheon, Korea, after 14 days at sea! It was quite a ride. As the LTs went ashore, I couldn't help thinking about our brothers who were stuck out in low tide like sitting ducks.

On arriving on shore, we had to muster up and gather for induction. There was a strange, temporary rule in place where everyone's rank was 0. Regular rank would resume when we left.

Talking about rank, I was waiting for my Sec. 4 promotion, but it never came. Then a Colonel got up and gave a speech, saying, "You gentlemen are sand bags here to hold back the enemy until replacements come. Because of the Geneva Conventions, we are allowed only 50 rounds of ammo."

What the hell are we going to do with only 50 rounds? I wondered. *We can maybe only handle two of the enemy with 50 rounds.*

So, my next destination was the 51st Signal Battalion I Corps, located in the same place as TV's M.A.S.H — Uiongbu, Korea. I hopped the train as instructed, and rode for what seemed like endless hours. It was a slow train that the Japanese had built. Finally, the conductor yelled out "Uiongbu!" (we-jom boo), and I got off in the middle of nowhere!

I waited 10-15 minutes, then suddenly in the distance I saw the Jeep that would take me to my new home. I reported to my new boss and was shown to my own office. There, I met the three clerks who would become my buddies.

After we got to know each other, they all gathered in my room and we had a BS session. It was lots of fun. We had the radio on and lis-

Soldier Boy in Peace Time

tened to Pyongyang Sally, or as we called her, "The Voice of Peking." Boy she was deceitful and convincing, sort of like our politicians today!

My job was to draw maps that showed the location of our DF Finders. The job of the DF Finders was to jam the north Koreans while on the move. To do my job, I needed a top-secret clearance. Talk about a grey area! The general wanted me to draw up a tactical schematic. The problem was I needed a Krypto Clearance, to do this which I didn't have.

It would take about a month to get the clearance, and it was against Army regulations to do the work without it, but the general insisted. He told my leader that I must do the job! "Jock," my nickname at this point, "you do it right away!" my boss said. "It's up to you. I'll back you up."

So, I said, "The General wants it, so it shall be!" I didn't get into trouble! Yay!

Now I want to talk about my buddies. My replacement came early. His nickname was Tex, because he was from Beaumont, Texas. He was married, and like me he stayed a "virgin" (faithful to his wife) for 14 long months.

Then there was Cob from New York. He graduated from NYU with a business degree. He liked to tease Tex and me about how gratifying it was to have a moose (a profession woman, if you know what I mean). He also regaled us with lots of personal info about his exploits in that area. Ha-ha! We looked at him as a joke, but he was a good guy.

Next was Neil, my best buddy. We would save each other's butts if we had to. He liked to play the piano. When he got to playing one of his concertos, he would stop in the middle and refuse to go on — temperamental artist! Another habit he had was he would spend all his pay before the end of the month. One time, he sold me his new camera for less than he paid for it because he ran out of money.

Then there was Norman. He was quite an accomplished artist who had taken a Norman Rockwell correspondence course. In fact, he resembled Rockwell. He did a great job sketching the Korean women. We would also exchange art.

The Korean women were fine looking, but when the American Doughnut Dollies were there, it was so great to see women from home! Boy, when they came around, in our minds we were back home for a few moments. It was kind of like a visit from Santa Claus.

A funeral crashed through our gate one day. By law, you can't stop or interfere with a Korean funeral in any way. It turned out the whole presentation was for a specific GI to observe. His moose had committed suicide because he was going home to his wife and kids!

So, her Korean mother and father demanded that he see what his plan to leave did to their daughter, his moose. I sure would've hated to be in his shoes. Apparently, suide was a common occurrence here when a moose had been exclusive with a GI who decided to go home rather than stay there with her.

After that scene, I have to go do my duty (poop), but I'm not going to sit on a log! I snuck into an officer's head (bathroom). These were located in a tent and had wooden seats, and they were *not* for EMs. Wouldn't you know it, as I sat down, the Colonel came in! He said, "HF Jock! How's it going?"

Sounding like a little boy caught doing something he shouldn't be, I said, "I hope you're doing great, sir. See ya." I got the hell out of there like my butt was on fire!

The first 12 months in Korea were good. It was easy duty, and fun. Us and our other buddy, Cookie, who had his own room, would play music together. The group of us had a band of sorts. Neil would play the piano, with me on the bongos and cook singing. Cookie also did a sketch of me that was pretty good. A 5th of Vodka was our beverage of choice for these get-togethers!

It's beautiful here in Korea! My buddy and I took a stroll to the village market to just look around. Boy, you can smell the charcoal burning along with other pungent odors. Speak-

Soldier Boy in Peace Time

Sketches

My friend, Neil.

Soldier Boy in Peace Time

My sketch of a Korean shoe shine boy.

Frank Di Giacomo

Sketch of a truck, Korea March 18, 1961.

Soldier Boy in Peace Time

Scenes from the Village

Frank Di Giacomo

ing of smells, the stench of kimchi is prevalent too — that's one distinct smell. Ugh!

Glancing over to one of the stands, I saw something that will be with me forever — a dog hanging there with his fur removed, ready to be butchered. No way!

When we headed back to base, we decided to take a short cut through the rice paddies. As we made our way through, we beheld another surprise — an umbilical cord and more stuff which I won't mention!

We had many practice alerts. I decided to be funny during one of them. Everybody else ran to the bunker to pick up a riffle and fully dress, but not me. I came out in boxer shorts! The Sergeant gave me heck for it, so I told him, "In combat, all I need is my rifle!" That did not go over well.

Then there was the time I stole the Colonel's Jeep and my buddies and I went to I-Corps to drink and raise cane! On the way back, we had a practice alert and I had to get the Jeep back!

As we came into the drive, the Colonel was standing there ready to jump in the Jeep. That time, my buddies disappeared and left me to take the blame for the crime. Thanks, guys!

The Colonel said, "Let's go, soldier!"

I said in a sheepish voice, "Sir, I don't have a military license!"

"I don't give a damn," he said loudly, "hit it!"

Frank in craft shop.

About that time, I almost had my pants full. Suddenly, the actual driver come rushing out, thinking he was late. Well, I got the hell out of there real quick!!!!

We had a craft shop owned by the military that had a GI manager named Sam. He was ready to go home, so he asked me to take over. I said okay and was happy to get extra money from taking over. I love to build and fly model airplanes, so it worked out fine and it was fun.

I was quite good at flying. I could go through all the maneuvers except the Cuban 8. Now

Frank with a model of a Russian Yak.

here's the fun part, I was flying a model of a Russian aircraft on U-control (a wire). It was time for Revelry, but the flag bearers had to wait until the plane ran out of gas before they could raise the flag.

This was another of my stunts that didn't go well. What I didn't know at the time was a Korean worker was watching me fly the model. The Russian plane with a red star on it looked just like the plane that wiped out his whole family. I felt bad when I found about that, and was truly sorry.

I missed home, my young wife and our 6-month-old son. I was sitting alone at Debby's bar, 8,000 miles away listening to "A Summer Place" and drinking lots of beer. This was long before cellphones, texting, Facetime and instant communication. It had been 14 months since I'd seen my family, which meant that letters were like candy to a baby! Thankfully, my mom and my wife wrote to me almost every day.

The holidays were an even worse bummer, especially Thanksgiving! I remember after having a good meal that day, I was sitting there alone since all the others had gone to spend time with their moose friends. It was quiet and all of a sudden, I felt extremely lonely. I imagined Mom, Dad, my sister Connie, and my brother and his wife and my niece and nephew all sitting around joking and laughing after polishing off a wonderful Thanksgiving meal. My eyes got watery.

It was also sad when I was having lunch in the field and we'd been instructed to not give the Korean children any of our food. I couldn't stand it when a little boy begged me to give him something, so I said, "Shhh! Don't tell anybody," and gave him some food anyway. I thought feeding one child at a time was better than none.

Christine, Cob's moose, was having a birthday party so all my buddies and were invited. It was great, and so was the food — especially because there was no kimchee! Thank God. Otherwise, we'd have to hold our noses.

After my tour of duty, I found out that Cob and Christine were going to get married. I think they stayed in Korea. I didn't see them again.

Me and my buddies went on a tour to the DMZ (demilitarized or neutral zone). There was a North Korean guard there who was standing and sweating in the sun because he was wearing a winter uniform in April. Further down the DMZ, I began to act up again. (What's new? ha-ha) I just had to step over the DMZ line. Why? Because I could! I stepped back, teasing the guard. Of course, I said a few choice words too.

I realized that really wasn't cool when the red guard pointed his AK 47 at my buddies when he saw what I was doing. My friends yelled, "Jock, stop it! Come back over here." So, I did. I could have started an international incident and been shot dead! Looking back, I realize I was not being cool.

On the way back, we had to cross over a bridge that was mined by the U.S. There were no pictures allowed here, so as a result, cameras were confiscated. I hid mine so I'd have a top-secret souvenir! When I got to a dark room, I discovered the film had been exposed to light! I hate when dat happens. Serves me right!

We were preparing for a parade formation at the same place where I flew my model. Each time we did this, the area had to be surveyed, and I helped to survey every time because the lieutenant hated the job. I suggested that after the survey was done we should place coffee cans filled with cement and paint them to mark the boundaries, this way we wouldn't have to do it every time. He thought that was a great idea and thanked me.

Now this only happens in the movies, but I just have to tell you about it. There was a semi on the field with four officers plus Major Mears inside. The Major, for some reason, called for me, so I reported in.

Shockingly, he asked me to take his place rather than asking one of the officers! I couldn't believe he would choose me, a PFC, over three Captains and a Lieutenant! *No way*, I thought, but did everything that was asked with more caution than usual. I was more of a secretary, which I think is safer. As a result, the officers gave me a good report.

It was cold one day in the field and our salamander shut down. Me and another guy got into our sleeping bags to stay warm and fell asleep. When I woke up, there was ice formed on the floor, ceiling, and both walls. I remember how numb I was from the cold. You think you should get up and move in this type of situation, but you don't because it's so darned cold. You know what I mean? I can tell you this, it gets cold in Korea and it's a cold that pierces right through you!

Another time in the field, the stairs on our sig van broke! We didn't have a welder and there were no maintenance men. We were going to have inspection real soon, so I had to think of something to get this fixed real fast.

I got some signal communication wire and wrapped it around the holes in the stairs and the truck frame. This is strong stuff. I tested the stairs and I was relatively sure it was safe. Even

Soldier Boy in Peace Time

so, when the Colonel climbed up the stairs, we held our breath! It all worked out, and this type of quick thinking is why I think the officers liked me. When they wanted something done, they called on me.

One day when I was taking a shower, I saw the Master Sergeant's back and it was scarred all to hell. I asked him what happened, thinking he might have been captured by the Japs. "No," he said, "that happened in combat. I finally shot him. Don't ever try to bayonet an Asian soldier, 'cause you'll fail!

I know what he means now. I was fooling around with Corporal Lee, who happened to be a Katusa (an elite Korean soldier), and he had me down in five seconds flat. (The regular solider is called Rock Army.)

A little about our quarters. When I first arrived, we lived in a Quonset hut, then shortly after we had a permanent block building.

One time when I was on guard duty, an MP pulled over a GI. The MP was polite but the GI resisted and that was it. The tough guy got the hell beat out of him! Moral to this story: if an MP pulls you over, be nice for your own good. (The MP was the same guy I threaten when we were marching. Small world!)

R&R in Japan, here I come! I headed out on a C47 "goony bird" — that's what they call the twin prop airplane that was the workhorse of the Army. When I got there, I was surprised by how the natives there treated us like kings. You'd think they would hate with losing the war and all, but that was not the case.

Osaka was the first city we went to. Our first stop was the USO. I thumbed through an address book there, and to my surprise I saw my uncle Stan Shor's name. Surprising and made me homesick!

Then my buddy and I buzzed to Tokyo and saw the Imperial Hotel. We also saw a live stage show. What's neat was the mike we wore translated things to English! The Ginza is like Broadway and they have a building with four floors of nothing but cameras.

Everything there is fast — taxicabs and trains. I have to say their trains are lower than ours! For a non-Christian nation, they sure act like they are one. They are honest to a fault. I never got cheated while converting yen to our dollar. They had police on every corner and the women, let's just say you won't be homesick. I recommend Japan.

After getting back and winding down, the Chaplains were having a clean speech contest for the best poster. So, I was asked to join. Guess what! I won first prize of the whole far east. My picture was seen in the Korean newspaper and *Stars and Stripes!*

Wow — I'm famous! Ha-ha.

Defcon One!

Suddenly, the honeymoon was over for us! There was a Defcon One alert, meaning the North Koreans had crossed the DMZ. They were really coming to shoot us! And we get only 50 rounds of ammo according requirements of the Geneva Conventions.

There was so much confusion. People were running in all different directions, and a couple of Sergeants were crying, saying, "This is how the conflict started back in 1950." Most also kicked out their moose companions, which seemed inhumane! Those girls were good enough for 13 months and now they were treating them like shit and all of a sudden, they want to see their wives and children.

You have to realize, when you go into battle you always like to think you have a chance of coming back alive. But for us, with only 50 rounds of ammo, we were sure it was sudden death for us.

Crazy me, I ran toward the guard house where the enemy would strike. I took cover

Soldier Boy in Peace Time

behind the head (toilets) and set my M2 carbine to single shot, thinking, *I only have enough ammo to kill 50 Gooks.* The small amount of ammo really played havoc with my mindset.

With no way to contact loved ones, we were all sure they wouldn't know what had happened to us. I had sent my last letters to my wife and Mom but I later found out they didn't get them.

Now as I look back, I think it was better that they didn't get those letters filled with doom and gloom. Mom wouldn't have been able to take it if she thought she'd lost me after she'd already lost her brother in WWII. It would have been too much.

All of a sudden, a miracle happened. The 7th Division wiped out the enemy before they could attack our location. Thank you, Lord! Shortly after that, and it was about time, we were headed home. YAY!

When I got tonsillitis, the medics picked me up to take me to the a hospital for treatment. When I got inside the truck, it was full of Turks!

I asked, "You guys play football? That seemed to be the sport you played while you were banging my shoulder." They are robust people and good allies.

One time when we were out in the field inside our sig van, our Sergeant was telling us that when he enlisted, he was in a plane flying with two military pilots. All of a sudden, a German ME BF109 airplane was having a great time sinking bullets all over the plane he was in. He said he could still hear the sound of the bullets coming through the thin sheet metal of the plane's walls. No question, all three of them had to bail out! He said the pilots had to struggle to get the him to put on his gear.

Another time at breakfast, I was in line with fussy, spoiled GIs that liked complaining to the cook. They'd say, "I don't want greasy eggs" or "My yoke is broken," etc. So, when it was my turn, me being me, I said, "Sarg, give me six eggs, greasy as hell with the yokes broken!"

Cookie said, "You going to eat six eggs?"

I said, "Watch me!" When I was done, I held up my empty tray.

After that, every time I showed up, he'd ask. "Six eggs?"

I'd answer, "No, just three today. I'm not too hungry."

Now my tour of duty wasn't all that bad. I remember being on Hill 500, sitting on the ledge. I said to my buddies Neill and Tex, "Just imagine swinging on a sky hook and just at that moment, we all got light headed. We agreed, it was time to go back."

Shipping Out!

I was finaly getting ready to ship out! It was sad saying goodbyes to all of my buddies and some officers who thought I should come back and take OCS, but that was the furthest thing from my mind.

We were going back on the USS *Patrick* and boy did it look great! There was joy all over the ship, even the Marines lightened up a bit. Ha-ha!

I got to get my sea legs back. I loved being outside watching the waves hitting the bow, and sitting under the exhaust fan on a chilly day.

Well at two days out, all of a sudden, I noticed the engine screws had stopped! *What the hell is going on?* I wondered. Fifteen minutes later, the skipper came on the PA and announced, "There's a Far East alert! So, we are headed for Laos!" Ouch! We all lost our joy mo-jo at that point!

The joy was replaced by the dead look we all suddenly had on our faces. The first thing that came to my mind was, *I was lucky in the first alert. Would I be lucky again? Christ, I haven't even seen my son yet and I haven't seen my loved ones for 14 months.*

Soldier Boy in Peace Time

We were getting close to our destination and then it happened! We were told that the Marines had stopped all the insurgents! This was the beginning of the Vietnam conflict.

There was one more week at sea and then I'd finally be off this boat. I didn't want to see the ocean again for a long while. But boy did that Golden Gate Bridge look good. It was the greatest sight I'd ever seen because it meant we were finally in San Francisco!

It took a whole day to muster out. My New York buddy scheduled a flight to Chicago where we were hoping to get a jet flight (a big deal, since jets were new at this point), but no luck. We ended up having to take a turbo prop. instead. The flight took seven hours, and that was with a favorable tail wind.

Well that's the end of my soldier's story but not the end of this book!

Present Day

At this writing, I'm 88 years old and to this day on Memorial Day, I always think of all of my brothers in arms who sacrificed for the good of our great country, which is the best one in the world. I also think of my dear Uncle Tony (my son's namesake), and remember him fondly.

Frank Di Giacomo

Tony had an outgoing personality, and he was a little crazy. (Ha-ha! Yes, I know who I take after.) His job in the Army Air was to drive the Colonel around. Being who he was, he wanted action instead! So, he asked the Colonel if he could go for training to be a turret gunner on a B-24. He got his wish.

He graduated gunner school and was assigned to the 866th Tech Training Squadron. He flew 25 missions and lived to tell the tales — no small feat! When he could have come home to his fiancé, he instead decided to stay because a gunner was needed. So he went for his 26th mission. Knowing him, I'll bet he volunteered. Unfortunately, his luck ran out on this mission and he lost his life.

He was reported as "missing in action." It turned out that this wasn't quite true, but it took me 80 years to find out the whole truth. His plane was hit over Manilla. The pilot and co-pilot jumped out and left the crew on the damaged plane. There was a Japanese witness to the incident, and he said the plane exploded.

I'm glad to know that he was not captured by the enemy, tortured and executed, which was always my fear.

Well, I guess it's that time. I hope you enjoyed my story. It's the truth (to the best of my recollection), and I'm sticking to it!

Thank you for reading this book and God Bless. Oh! Do one me a favor, please! If you see a hungry Veteran, feed him, and if you see a Veteran who needs help, please help him.

Thank you again, and God Bless.

www.ingramcontent.com/pod-product-compliance
Lightning Source LLC
Chambersburg PA
CBHW040155020625
27551CB00048B/384